Words

Of

Rain

James Coburn

WORDS OF RAIN

COPYRIGHT ©2014 James Coburn

Printed in the United States of America

**ISBN-13:978-0692288580
(BlaqRayn Publishing Plus)**

ISBN-10:0692288589

Printed by Createspace 2014
Published by BlaqRayn Publishing in 2014

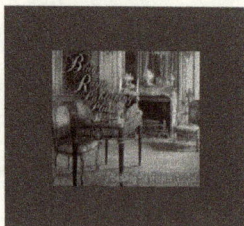

WORDS

OF

RAIN

James Coburn

Table of Contents

Words of Rain

Words of Rain

DEDICATION

*This book of Poetry is
dedicated to my Mother
Thelma Joslyn Coburn*

Acknowledgments

I thank the following persons for encouraging me along the way:

Mark Nottingham, Elizabeth Wylie, Jimmy Epperson, Paul Fairchild, Cheryl Hamilton, Carol-Cole Frowe, Andreas Gunzel, Alice Collinsworth and Jeremy Ferslew. Thank you Jimmy for our talk about the horizon and transcendence.

Many thanks to Daryl Halencak and Kevin Conner of Southwestern Recording Studio and KevyD Records for their gracious invitation in asking me to record "Words of Rain" as an audio book.

Thank you Kevin Conner for producing "Words of Rain" with original music of your own making. Daryl, you have a deep soul.

Generous appreciation goes to Kim Morrow of BlaqRayn Publishing.

❧

*Days are full of
dragons.
Nights are for rain.*

Words of rain.

❧

December Rose

Rose bud
never opened,
caught by winter.
A hint of red remains
in petals, barely unfurled.
So dry my finger breaks
those enfolding its core,
still holding tight, not to reveal
what fell from the clouds
to rise from earth and inspire
these words of rain.
There is no dogma
more meaningful than this
simple bud, left brittle
in late frost, returning
to earth in gentle course
with the wind.

Becoming Day

My first thought was of breath.
Inhale soulful vision, down to earth;
exhale for survival.
Was it the wind I felt upon my face
that February morning long ago,
going home
wrapped in mother's arms?
The wind linked to all the earth.
Earth waited eons for my view of
recognition.
Love was simple in the complexity
of reason.
For my mother's kindness did I
breathe,
create an imprint like no other.
You've found your vision, a prism of
light,
revealing colors, harmony of day
break
as seconds are newborn,
and lifetimes make entrances and
exits
between breaths.
Before, floating in the womb, an
ocean of creation,
I sensed exhilaration of speed,
as Nebulae smelted stars.

Crossing Cottonwood Creek

Country road
leads to a steel county bridge
where life settles in easy sway
of prairie grass.
Highway, miles away.
I take a road spanned by red hawks
and jack-rabbits,
A frantic city, left behind.
Box cars rumble through summer
wheat
as tons of steel cross horizon
with the weight of commerce
spinning beyond sight.
I'm homeless as rain
under a full moon
casting light on a trail.
I wander through a clearing
among crumbling farmhouses
that did not cage Depression-era folk
now forgotten.
Gray wood chips away.
Abandoned useless clutter.
Home for journeymen like me.
A sweep of memory
like wild crows free in the wind.
Far away clouds rise above 1930's
bridge,
creaking planks,

whispers of farmhands and poets.
Generations of song by old men,
hitchhikers and vagabonds.
Men whistled tunes, building this
bridge
to journey beyond the Great
Depression.

New generations search for words to
make sense
of the Great Recession;
foreclosures, mortgages under water.
So, I cross.
I turn to hear life listening to me.
And I see a road of red earth
cleared by young men,
for a better tomorrow.
Their love waits for them in a cool
oasis of white sheets falling like
clouds.
Unspoken dreams drift down

Cottonwood Creek
under footsteps crossing the narrow
bridge.
Wilderness follows the ancient
Cottonwood.
Jack rabbit
jumps as locusts
chirp an earthy buzz.
Just enough to turn the head

of a tom cat as I follow.
Soft paws - not a sound - scamper
around the bend;
wild as the horizon
calling me home.

Life Beside the Interstate

Life in splintered wood,
abandoned generations ago,
is home to restless ants gone picking.
Wild eyes mark your days;
days that passed generations of farm
folk
vanished in red earthy dust.
Jack rabbits blink. Nothing else;
No memories
of hands patching cotton shirts,
coffee brewing,
dresses made of feed sacks.
Loosened nails drop where
rusted barbed wire did not protect
them
from black blizzards, nor doubt.
Parents gathered goods,
Bon Voyage down Route 66.
Now a floor rots to the ground
amid the turnpike hiss.
Interstate crosses unmarked graves.
Dug-out cellar shelters coyote pups,
mother on the prowl.
This, too, will pass with a plaintive
howl,
fading across a prairie of bulldozers,
Wilderness grows in concrete cracks.

Rise from Ash

Life exposed to poets.
A rock embeds an imprint
known by a child flipping stones
tossing into river
or skimming a pond, sinking.
So the poet goes as fog
lifts from dark woods
leaving vapors dripping from limbs.
Wind falls, rushing November rose
for the last time,
the same wind that howls
through my window
before a frost.
So the earth lets go.
Clouds rise and the ground quakes;
fire licks fallen leaves.
Seedlings rise from ash
as a lone elk crosses the trail
unscathed, upward bound.

Steps

I am born by spirit
where I transcended within the
womb
to warm myself amid the ashes.
I burned. Set myself in celestial
flame
to cool. But my cool is another man's
pain.
His mine, unless I dance with the
phoenix
rising from the flame.

Followers for a Narcissist

They are the keepers of myth
morphing fear into invention
of some disposable god
thrust high in the heavens
above common misconceptions.
They are known by red hawks
under a hot August moon
making a nest on a pinnacle
known by a few at first
then by many as their exit looms.
They grapple with revolution
as kingdoms fall
leaving room for heroes
and the mainstream to rise
from muck.

Morning Ritual

Across from you
before your silver reflection, your
face
in a tug of war of want and fear,
lashing out with your eyes,
but consoling with your lips
that open for a Greek god's poetry
of myth and heroes in a world
that does not listen.
And all your forms conspire
to evoke a curious stare
as you perform your ritual of dress
running your hand through your hair
to feel.

Out of Eden

They seem as cave creatures
in their clans
to expel those unlike them.
So ancient in instinct
they abandon intuition
to kill neighbors beyond the hill
looking for berries or a warm fire.
Now they order nations
from caves of marble edifice.
They rule with dogma
killing earth for self.

Into Eden

Farewell to madness,
to news torching peaceful shade.
No complaint of autumn coming,
after August stripped
elm branches bare.
Before the last leaf falls,
I will spend my days in the woods,
or safe in a field I knew as a boy;
monarchs and wild blackberries,
violet wildflowers
beside cool canopy of creek-side
oaks.
Branches mingle there sending
roots deep in soil,
exploring what no one sees.

Metamorphosis

Let us become rain for a night,
permeate surface dragons,
dashing their fire.
Let thunder pass between us
as we seep down shingles,
to window pane cracks
and fall deep into mountains;
mix with seascapes.
Trickle down a mailbox
into a letter we would have written,
had it not been for the dragons.
Let all the words ever spoken
be drenched by rain.
Let rivers of ink flow down pages
and decay into earth.
Life will rise where we fell
wilted in spring rain.
Bees will hover above us
in scents of honeysuckle
where wilderness beckons.
We will bead dust where others walk
above surface dragons
fading into water
for millenniums.

House of Vines

When you wind down to sleep,
think of a window in Paris
overlooking a garden view.
Vines stretch green in shade
up building where passing
lives have lived.
We met in a trance
of watercolors
drenching dry paper.
Never a gardener seen,
only our view breaking day.
At night we crossed the Seine,
walked through Le Mariais
with our candle dream.
Old cafe conversations
sent secrets in the air.
But never a day spent from view
of the old garden from yesteryear.
Now I tend it in my dreams
with my friend beside me
so it seems.
Vines wrap around our path.

Walking in Paris

Master of watercolors
crosses the River Seine.
Water laps beneath our stride
on stones arranged by thought,
one-by-one.
Andreas in black strikes a match.
Gargoyles of Notre Dame dress in
blue-gray.
Alley cat slips between courtyard
gate.
Candles flicker in windows along
Les Marais.
Love in rare form,
never alone.
I know the end of gentle rain.
Where trains pass by in the night.
Footsteps pace down Le Marais
as days shift down the Seine.

Remnants of Day

Words are all I have this December
morning.
Bag pipes of New York City clear the
air
as I walk down sidewalks with and
without you,
waiting for you,
remembering our days.
Poinsettia in the window.
Christmas dinner on a table
found abandoned in Soho on a winter
day.
We never spoke after you went away
after our promise.
I never meant for my words to be our
last song,
whispered across city-scape.
Intersections come. We vanish from
view
on sidewalks of rustling leaves.
Words are all I have.

Night Watch Along the Deep Fork

Stretch your claws with me
beside the river tonight.
Flabby flip toads will entertain us.
There's a slicked-back honky cat I
know.
From the alley way we see
Kitty Cat-Caty dashing to join us
as the door flies open,
and two-legged cow chasers call
him.
Make way for tall grass to hide us
amid gossiping toads
bellowing about bouncing bugs.
Deep Fork is rising with crawdads
where some of those two-legged
cow chasers dropped smelly fish.
Hush. Big slobber-tooth broke his
leash,
barks from the alley
with tongue dripping and nose
sniffing.
Make our way in moonlight
to old boards with beetles,
cracks with hiding places
between jumps.
Share some of that big-ear squeal
stuck in your claws.

Words of Rain

Scamper now while
another cow chaser whistles
for his thick-skull buffoon
gnawing dead cow bones.
Flabby flip toads splash
for our high jump back to the grass.

Maple Street

Hammer Jacks built my home
pounding nails, pitching a frame.
1901 corner house has stood,
absorbing 11 decades of talk.
Men pulled rope for window ballasts,
tight, but loose as their dreams.
Gone now.
Young men became yesterday.
at this door.
Layers of white paint on scuffed
woodwork,
dented days
from fervor joining rooms,
spurred by eyes on the miller's
daughter
across the road.
Stares studded like nails
for the miller's barefoot blue-eyed
daughter.
A slam of wood, a break for water.
Sweat from inborn heat.
Tess pumped a bucket of spring
water
splashing as she crossed the road.
Her eyes on a carpenter,
His locks of dark hair dripped salty
beads.
Tess turned to walk home, but not
away

and the carpenter knew it;
The miller's blue-eyed daughter.
Upstairs, a room with a view, a turret
upward bound, where strong backs
never yield.
Come again at midnight
a road to cross to a turret of
moonlight.

Ballad of Joe and Misty Sue

Young farm hands a humming.
Okie storm's a coming.
Purple skies mixed with gray,
drench prairie bales of hay.
Country boys work all day, love all
night
save their pennies for Okie life.
Across the bridge of Cottonwood
Creek
Joe left his love under white sheets.
Lightening splinters across the sky;
green twigs in red dust fly by.
Joe's long legs are running,
His newly-wed heart's a thumping.
Joe leaps through a field
of ready-to-harvest wheat;
cyclonic wind can't be beat.
Crosses his heart in slanting rain,
knowing life without Misty ain't the
same.
When ya work all day, romp all night
ya need some prayers to set life right.
Joe loved all night with Misty Sue.
What else is a country boy to do.
But then, oh misery --
not a dime in his blue jean pants.
So work a day extra by chance,
'til raging storm disaster
breaks Joe's walls of plaster.

Words of Rain

Wind kicks Joe through front door
panting for breath, lungs sore.
Life's got reckoning to do.
Old farm dog shows wet nose
from under a blanket and Misty's
clothes.
Joe searches for Misty Sue.
To a storm cellar, she already flew.
Still simmering on stove is chicken
soup
as he runs through "balk, balk,"
chicken coupe.
Dashes with his yellow lab;
lifts shelter door to something sad.
Misty's arms wrapped around Johnny
Blue
after telling Joe, "I'll be lonesome for
you."
Johnny and Misty kissed all day,
romped passed noon,
got naked in the morning dew.
Joe caught Johnny with Misty Sue.
What else for a friend named Blue.
For two fellers across the range,
simple lives without a lick of change,
there's some expense with Misty Sue.
Life's got reckoning to do.

View from a Box Car

Around the hour of midnight,
I keep writing, writing a circus of
words.
Step right up hooligans dangling legs
from Ferris wheel.
Board passenger train left abandoned
where the road ends
in view of an old pick-up truck
where clothes shuffle in night's
breeze.
Down the road, a woman on a
balcony stretches
a leg from porch swing.
Lamps behind flimsy curtains click
off
for a face peering from behind
smudgy window pane.
Old nosy Parker's eyes chase gum
chewing skateboarder
crossing Harrison Street at daybreak.
Wet smell of railroad cars mixes a
cocktail
of empty graffiti walls, a broken
chair and torn packages,
beside crunched beer cans and
cigarette butts
that once meant something to
someone.
Steel wheels smooth from spinning,

glare past
every guilty sin of innocents pressing
heaven or hell.
But they are only words, written on
pages
to be forgotten by darkened streets.

Magnetic Verse

My need for electric skies
splinters across midnight sea
a call from Elysian fields.
An elemental, magnetic verse
known by the tides and jungle
orchids
opens a bohemian dream, finding
self
in an ocean greater than self,
becoming self.
Pathway swallows stars beyond
breath,
streaking stardust inside out.
Awakened, I touch petals deep blue,
edges tinged red,
and burn bright beyond haze.

Hollow Wood

My soul, deep in memory
has lived many Septembers
as nature's force wilted the moon
flower,
drooping for younger blossoms
to fill with nectar for bees.
Vines trace the journey of trees
spreading their branches.
Such is life in cadence with the stars
to shine on lovers' new days
in a frequency we witness and live
until snow melting on winter grass
uncovers a man, hollow as fallen
elms,
a space now empty as ant trails
within moon flower vines,
giving back to the earth his yield.
But there is always sky, wind as free
as thought, swirling around
city-scapes
and canyons, lifting red hawks to sail
in spirit wind, free to live where an
updraft
settles wings to nest.

Night Must Fall

Fragments of loneliness
cross strands of green embroidery
on a chair rocking beside bay
window.
Mantle clock ticks in cadence
of alley cat crossing Maple Street.
Plaintive call
penetrates broken stained glass,
his sanctuary of night.
Variegated bits of moonlight cross
room
where I dream of mist beckoning
waves of violet canyon light.
Chaco Canyon bowl spins.
Candle light flickers on aqua
coastline brushstrokes.
Turquoise-gray tide splashes
intransigent rocks.
Words of rain fall one-by-one from
bookshelf,
lifted by wind to touch my face.
My moment of time, suspended.
Intensity of color with earth's
rotation.
Candlewick smolders amid hush of
night.
Depth of creation pulled by sister
moon
vibrates ebb tide flow,

rushing my feet, absorbing my steps.
Tiger sun rises over ocean of life.
Endless waves crest before horizon
as rising sea reflects in my eyes,
envisioning soul.

Prairie Grass Boy

Violet wildflower of boyhood,
I found you in field of prairie grass
near a canopy of Cross Timbers
spanning
Deep Fork Creek.
I reached down to pick you,
twirling stem in fingers, brushing my
nose.
A flower not much larger than my
thumb,
near to the milkweed's leaves that
felt
like a cat's tongue.
Underground spring trickled down
ant trail
with a petal it carried away
down flooded earthen cracks.
Prairie soul seeps with life
into decades as I am washed
by a river of no return.

Journey of Souls

So long ago a gentle wind
asked my name.
The first day blue eyes saw snow
Cast endlessly from our childhood
door.
Sisters press their noses.
On foggy glass window panes.
Dash outside mittens pulled off
after my mother opens snow banked
door.
I met this fresh air in sudden breath.
Bare swish through snow.
Now I see days lifting as she smiles
with the joy of what has been.
I'm not afraid to die, she says.
I remember
fields of snow on golden grass
spanning past ancient creek bed
of protruding bones canopied by
Redbud
branches pressed to the ground.
Worry fades in glistening blue light.
Pools of water lift souls
to windswept flight where redbirds
color night with a gathering of souls.

Becoming Self

With one thought.
I became a distillation,
a landscape
for those who sleep, touch deeply.
Inside ferments everyone I've
known;
universes, collapsed spaces,
water spilling through worm holes
and out to sea with ebb tide moon.
Deep blue heaven
is where peace and kindness are one
with all I have been
on this epoch journey
of self.

Spirit Wind

Storms darken red rock canyon,
scattering life into caves.
Kneeling, an ancient one follows the
storm
as mystic light splinters above land
and drops of rain trickle in clay pots.
Wild gray hair fallen on bronze
shoulders,
her eyes trace the land she knows.
The last of her kind,
she hears spirit voices rise in wind,
in cadence with the steps a lone gray
wolf,
stopping to drink where ancestors
roamed.
Flood swells beyond embankment of
fresh pools.
An eagle watches from her perch.
White whiskered alpha presses earth,
presses death.

Stardust Creation

He breathes universe pulsing
microwaves,
vibrations clashing in gases,
a big bang
never heard by man,
compressed and discovered
by intuition
or technology for radio listeners
on their morning drive.
Life in micro flashes.
He marks time, bending in worm
holes
unaware that he crawled out of
himself,
breaking away from defensive rants
of surface cannons.

With a blink he searches a hum
found between wild emerald green,
reddest red.
He breathes in obscure earth, wet
with life,
primal core.

A tree fell in the forest
to decay amid a micro flash of
spiraling sounds.
Evolution of soul
meshed with vibrations left silent in

another frequency.
Only flashes between breaths
until he recognizes his own voice.

Invitation to Day

Thought I'd drop by this old place.
Wanted to see if any laughter
survived
walking through this door.
Oh how much you wanted out of life;
this funny world we live in.
Nice to meet you some day.
Don't mind me, we've met before
in those dreams of what would be,
couldn't be, told not to be for me.
But I stepped out for a new day to
last,
so that's why I've come here to say
it's Okay. Your world slipped by, but
I met mine. And no flit of the tongue
or trail across gloom can take away
all this joy.
Not the longest night or cold winter
rain
will stop me now. For this day is
blessed,
each moment caressed by my own
way.
His voice in Paris. Her voice in May.
Into the depths I've seen all the love
a man can know. Must be the
beginning.
Nothing owed to the fates of
passersby.

Words of Rain

They made their choices and I've
made mine.
Nothing more than love will shine.
Nothing less than love will invite my
day.
For nothing less than love will I stay.

Blending Colors

Sisters teased their hair,
painted their faces black, their lips
white.
Faces like a black and white
television set.
Northeast Oklahoma City, 1963.
Feet jigged to Dixieland jazz.
rehearsing a minstrel show.
Parents laughed in school auditorium
until learning black children enrolled
there.
A young black girl on the school bus
was called "Big Bertha".
Nobody asked for her real name.
She sat alone, looking up beyond
window.
Birds of autumn crossed fall sky
blended with horizon of color.
Black families crossed
long-established boundaries
There was a dream,
a dream for people of color
to live in harmony.
White flight filled the suburbs
searching for a white spot in the
universe.
Courthouses divided bathrooms.
Hospital entrances were reserved for
whites.

"You can't bring them in this way," a
physician said.
Still, people forget.
They forget the danger of ignoring
history
unless the history compliments them.
Laws created two societies,
one colored or negro,
everybody else white.
People are less intolerant,
but some were never challenged
by new ideas.
Flocks of birds cross the sky.
Colors blend in southern horizon.
to find warm oasis.

Oklahoma Lynching

Mosquitoes tasted blood of white
men
standing shoulder-to-shoulder across
the Cimarron River bridge.
Separation of color in black and
white, west of Okemah.
A postcard reveals the 1911 mob
lynching;
Laura Nelson and son Lawrence, 15,
hanged from bridge.
Dead wooden planks, dry under
footsteps.
I bet a few the 50 spectators
photographed the next morning
dragged mother, infant and son from
court house jail.
Distant faces exposed to curious
stare.
Sunday communion trickled blood of
Christ touching lips.
Mosquitoes swarmed down river.
Infant missing.
Communion quenched killers'
Sunday best.
Murder played God.
White hands gripped rope tight to
Laura's neck after gang rape.
Lawrence shoved from bridge.
Slam of gravity forces pants to

dangle under naked feet.
Mosquitoes swarm down river,
Skim the edge, fester torch light of
malice.
Muted faces of men, women and
children
Stood gripping iron laced bridge a
century ago.
You lynchers, dead now with your
waters of injustice.
I spit in your waters. I drink of
justice for mother and son.
They said Lawrence, 15, shot Sheriff
Loney in the leg.
They said a posse went with Loney
to investigate a cow theft.
Lawrence saw the sheriff draw a
weapon.
His father pleaded guilty to the theft;
taken to prison.
Laura pled guilty to save Lawrence,
a false trigger of hope.
Postcards sold like slavery. Image
now free.
Mosquitoes swarm down the river,
skim the edge, fester torch light of
malice.

Hank

My father barely spoke a word.
I heard him roll rubber bands
down inky, dry newspapers;
saw him sip black coffee,
while covered in wheat dust,
pass communion,
read books of the wild West.
I didn't know much about him,
but knew everything he could give
across a big wooden desk.
Sharing work lunch,
his white coffee cup stained.
Silent laughter, clear blue eyes
for cameras, developing
photographs.
Can a smile be so quiet?
First of nine children to come,
he spoke of his parents.
1920's belongings weighed down
their truck,
chugging up river, crossing a dried
up river
somehow. I never knew.
His father headed for the oil fields
of Drumright.
At 57, Hank's arms shoveled flood
water
from windows under empty wheat
bins.

Words of Rain

Rubber boots sloshed toward
scampering rats,
squeaky gray belts caked in dust,
dead spiders clinging to cob webs.
Wheat dust in nostrils, brown beads
of spit.
On weekends, he lifted me in his
arms,
from a white 1959 Pontiac,
putting me in bed after drive-in
movie.
Rustling leaves, fireflies and
crickets.
Few words spoken the next morning.
I couldn't call him "Dad." Others
called him "Hank."
He taught me to ride a bike
the summer day he pounded nails in
a roof.
But his silence made life bittersweet;
silence as dark as the universe I
question.
I held his hand, taking me outside
my 5-year-old self
to the highest edge of the grain
elevator.
No rail.
He jumped on box cars rolling with
wheat,
turned the brake, started the auger.
I did the same at 19. Harvest

mornings into night
Sixteen hours of sweat.
My bare shoulder,
a ledge for rats in concrete tunnel.
Jumping on upward bound pulley,
my feet off the brakes, hands on
rope.
All quiet into winter as apricot tree
flowered in spring.
Rotten wheat bins to clean.
Solitary voice reverberated Macbeth
in bins of putrid air.
A shovel ready in the Cold War
fallout shelter.
Bombs never came, only fallout.
Dust. Alzheimer's disease.
Connections on riverbeds
receding from their banks.
"You're not James."
"I've lost my peace of mind."
"I've been to the moon."
My mother there with cancer.
"Let me know if there is anything I
can do," he said.
"I pray for you sometimes," he said
to me one night,
transcending between days of little
deaths.

WORDS OF RAIN

Life whispers
of canyons submerged in the sea
undiscovered, but known to creation.
Ancient gamma rays
never seen link to the grass.
Each grain of sand,
pulse of light known to me
touches life, touches day.
I will be with you because your days
are my days, our breaths, our own.
Pollen found deep under Antarctic
surface
melts my surface.
Rain forest particle now bound in
rock,
we have inhaled beneath same
ancient sun.
I am but a mixed palette of water
colors,
chosen chords from a harp,
random nights,
as I walk on land, speaking words of
rain
in desert lands, ice continents and
drought.
Yesterday I walked through a jungle
of moon flowers, breezy with bees
their own symphony of dance, air

Words of Rain

born
suckling water from earthy vines
as I moved in peace.

Room of Leaves

I remember how young weeds
would bend in wind
before brittle wildflowers crumbled.
I would imagine life
rising from that root,
a long way to go.
Summer seemed forever
until my boyhood friend left.
His blond hair faded
behind 1960 station-wagon glass
moving down the road.
I watched from my room of leaves,
drooping branches of Redbud tree.
I remember thinking that in this day,
now, the constant present,
I would remember
days piling with leaves,
unspoken words
of life blowing in the wind.

Birds of Autumn

Old man
carry a strand of torchlight
down to see the loons
gathering on woodland pond.
Dark autumn mist of gold
covers leaves melding into earth.
Night loons call before their journey
to spend winter on coastal waters.
Far away, with them you say,
you will go tomorrow
as ash becomes your flame
and your eyes join the heavens
in winged flight.

Worn Edges, Countless Days

Relentless writing
just as wind scatters leaves,
I stare into the horizon.
Pages saved, words wasted,
fever over spent.
My hand carries a book of poetry,
edges worn.
I hold a thousand days
from when we were young and full
of spark.
Your days became my days, the
flame
of smoldering wick, too bright for
words,
too dark for day.

Missing Nick

Morning rain turned to snow
outside my window.
You had perished, I read,
away from this frost.
I find it hard to write of snow
after words of rain dropped from
Elysian fields
ending drought.
Turning wind took your name.
All of your longings transcended
beyond days, as your brushstrokes
lingered dry in pentimento.
We never again shared lunch,
laughter among friends.
So went the day into darkest night,
fading beyond dusk into the shadows
you loved.
Seven moons led three white horses
to your boat
as oars thrust down the river Thebes,
sojourning where winter chill is
warmed by spring,
and rain nourishes the desert flower.

Love Not Lost

I trace how love fled;
doors shut in younger days.
Fear wept of illusion,
a silence I dared not speak,
seemingly forever;
but the rose of winter
with petals red
did not die before frost.
Its bud had not opened, was not lost.
By hand, pricked by thorn
I plucked winter's rose
to see petals open in form.

Twilight Journey

Take down this book at day's end.
Open where leaves were pressed,
yellow and red.
Pages stained by a heart of gold,
yet a journey to behold.
Let your eyes travel
to where the fog crept
gently across town
through window screens where she
slept
before you left for a day's work.
How many words were pressed
between your hands,
wrapped around your story
like a prayer?
Always searching
beyond the fireside's
last flame.
When robins take their last flight
before a winter's tale,
remember, it was your soul
lifting wings to sail.

About The Author

"Words of Rain" is Oklahoma poet James Coburn's first book of poetry. His poem "Oklahoma Lynching" was also published in "Elegant Rage" an anthology by Village Book Press celebrating the centennial birthday of Woody Guthrie.

More than once has Coburn been a selected poetry reader at the Woody Guthrie Festival in Okemah, Oklahoma as well as Oklahoma City.

His poetry has been published in poetryvlog.com and has appeared in anthologies published by the Poetry Society of Oklahoma.

In 2013, Coburn was awarded
membership in the Oklahoma
Journalism Hall of Fame.

He resides in Guthrie,
Oklahoma.

www.ingramcontent.com/pod-product-compliance
Lightning Source LLC
Chambersburg PA
CBHW031527040426
42445CB00009B/438